From Rags to Riches: The Wealth Whisperer's Secrets

Christopher D. Scott

INTRODUCTION.

We all aspire to wealth and financial success in the grand scheme of things. We long for a life in which our prosperity not only ensures our future but also gives us the freedom to pursue our aspirations. You'll go on a life-changing journey within these pages, following the fascinating tale of the journey from poverty to wealth.

Imagine living a life in which money serves as a tool to create opportunities rather than a cause of worry. Your guide to that world is this book. It's evidence of the effectiveness of planning and understanding—the very things that will enable you to open the doors to financial success.

We will delve into the mysteries of the Wealth Whisperer throughout these chapters. This mentor has helped innumerable people go from financial ruin to prosperity. The ideas and tactics discussed in these pages are tried-and-true methods that have helped regular individuals become wealthy success stories, rather than abstract theories.

Turn the pages to learn how to establish a strong financial foundation, define your financial goals, and develop a wealth-conscious attitude. You'll discover how to make prudent investments, manage your money, and successfully negotiate the complex world of real estate. These chapters give useful advice that you may incorporate into your journey, regardless of your goals—be they to become a successful business owner or to become an expert debt manager.

We'll also discuss the value of risk management and insurance in protecting your wealth, as well as the rewarding practice of giving back. Making a positive impact on the world is equally important as accumulating wealth on this trip.

The path to wealth is neither simple nor short, but it is reachable for those who are prepared to set out on it with a strong sense of resolve and an open mind. Your guide, The Wealth Whisperer's Secrets, will help you at every turn and arm you with the information, resources, and motivation you need to realize your financial goals.

Let us now embark on our journey. Flip the page, widen your thinking, and be ready to turn your life around from poverty to wealth. This is the beginning of your journey into the land of abundance and fortune.

Chapter 1

Defining Your Financial Goals.

Every effective journey starts with a well-defined endpoint in mind. Similar to how a ship needs a course to follow, having a clear set of goals is essential to achieving financial prosperity. This chapter will discuss the significance of establishing clear financial goals and how they can act as your compass when aspiring to become wealthy.

The Influence of Sense.

Consider that you have neither a map nor a GPS as you embark on a cross-country road trip. Even if you drive randomly, it's improbable that you'll end up where you're going. This also holds for your financial path. If you don't have specific, well-defined goals, your financial endeavors may be aimless and unfocused.

Establishing financial objectives gives you a path to accumulating wealth. It assists you in responding to important queries like:

•In terms of finances, what are your long- and short-term goals?
•What kind of lifestyle do you and your family have in mind?
•What type of retirement do you hope to have, and when do you wish to retire?
•Do you have any particular financial goals, such as launching a business, buying a house, or sending your children to college?

Understanding the answers to these queries is the cornerstone of your financial strategy. Your objectives will provide you with the drive and attention you require to continue on your current path in the face of obstacles.

Financial Goal Types.

Financial objectives fall into various categories:

1. Short-Term Objectives: These are usually objectives you wish to accomplish in the upcoming year or so. These may consist of setting up an emergency fund, eliminating high-interest debt, or setting aside money for a trip.

2. Medium-Term Objectives: These objectives include several years and could involve financing your child's education, saving for a down payment on a home, or purchasing a car.

3. Long-Term Objectives: These are usually the most important ones. Examples include building a sizable investment portfolio, setting aside a sizeable amount for your descendants, or saving for retirement.

Setting SMART Goals.

Use the SMART criteria to help you develop realistic financial goals:

- **Specific:** State your goals clearly in your head. Phrases like "I want to be rich" are not very helpful; instead, say something like, "I want to save $1 million."

- **Measurable:** Ascertain that your objectives are quantifiable. If your objective is to pay off debt, for instance, be specific about how much you wish to pay off.

- **Achievable:** Your objectives ought to be demanding but doable. While having lofty aspirations is admirable, your objectives should be attainable with patience and work.

- **Relevant:** Make sure your priorities and values line up with your aims. Within the framework of your life, they ought to make sense.

- **Time-Bound:** Give each aim a precise deadline. A deadline, no matter how long it is—one year or ten—creates accountability and a sense of urgency.

You have developed a strong compass that will direct your financial decisions and actions by defining your financial goals and adhering to the SMART criteria. It's the beginning of your road from poverty to wealth, and it establishes the parameters for all that comes after. Thus, give careful thought to defining and documenting your financial objectives. It will determine your future wealth.

We'll look at how your mentality can be an effective tool for accomplishing these objectives in the upcoming chapter.

Chapter 2

Mastering the Mindset of Wealth.

It's time to start working toward your financial goals now that you've established them. But without the correct attitude, even the most clearly defined objectives can remain unattainable. We will explore the crucial idea of developing a wealth mindset in this chapter.

The mental capacity.

Your financial ship is steered toward wealth or left adrift in an uncertain sea by your thinking, which is similar to that of a captain. Possessing a certain quantity of money is not what defines a wealthy mindset; rather, it refers to the way you see money and wealth in general.

Think about this: Negative money ideas, like "money is the root of all evil" or "I'll never be rich," have the potential to come true. On the other hand, you're more likely to make decisions and perform actions that result in financial success if you adopt an optimistic and powerful mindset.

Important Aspects of a Wealth Mentality.

1. Abundance Mentality: The emphasis of a wealth mindset is on abundance rather than scarcity. Instead of seeing barriers, it sees opportunity. It all comes down to having faith that there is enough money for everyone and that your success does not come at the expense of other people.

2. Financial Literacy: Gain knowledge about investments, money, and financial concepts. A wealth mindset is based on understanding. You'll feel more assured and in charge of your finances the more financial knowledge you possess.

3. Delayed Gratification: Disciplined, long-term actions are frequently the foundation of wealth building. Wealthy people understand that making some sacrifices now might pay off in the long run with bigger benefits. It has to do with putting future financial security ahead of gratification.

4. Risk Tolerance: A key component of a wealth mindset is being willing to take measured risks. This doesn't imply being careless, but realizing that some risk is required to achieve financial progress. Making educated decisions is more important than completely avoiding danger.

5. Goal-oriented: People with a wealth mindset are driven and goal-oriented. It helps you stay focused and motivated to constantly work toward your financial goals.

Getting Rid of Limiting Thoughts.

Many people have restrictive attitudes about money that stem from their upbringing or prior encounters. Some examples of these beliefs include: "I don't deserve wealth," "I'm not good with money," and "wealthy people are greedy." Identifying and disputing these notions is an essential first step toward cultivating a wealth mindset. Change them out for beliefs and affirmations that help you reach your financial objectives.

Attitude and Behavior.

It's critical to realize that having a wealth mentality involves more than just thinking positively; it also entails matching your beliefs to your behavior. Your way of thinking should enable you to make wise financial decisions, save, and invest to reach your financial objectives.

We'll go into doable methods for accumulating wealth in the next chapters, as well as how this wealth mindset may propel you from poverty to affluence. Keep in mind that your perspective serves as the compass that steers your financial ship, so make sure it leads you in the direction of the wealth and success you desire.

Chapter 3

Building a Solid Financial Foundation

Your financial success depends on a strong financial foundation, just like a robust structure needs a strong foundation. We'll look at the essential actions to create and preserve the base on which your wealth can be grown in this chapter.

<u>Creating Your Financial Foundation.</u>

Your financial base is comparable to a skyscraper's foundation. It must be strong, steady, and capable of bearing the entire weight of your financial objectives. **The following are the essential elements of creating a strong financial foundation:**

1. Emergency Fund: To begin with, establish an emergency fund large enough to cover three to six months' worth of necessities. This fund acts as a safety net in case of unanticipated events like job loss or medical issues.

2. Debt Management: Give paying off credit card debt and other high-interest debt top priority. Building a solid financial foundation requires first reducing and then paying off debt.

3. Budgeting: Create a spending plan that accounts for your earnings and outlays. This enables you to track your spending and make the required changes to invest and save money.

4. Savings strategy: Create a consistent savings strategy by allocating a portion of your income toward retirement, a down payment on a house, or education.

<u>The Value of Financial Knowledge.</u>

Financial literacy is one of the keystones of your financial foundation. It is not enough to just have money; you also need to know how to invest and grow it. **Some essential elements of financial literacy are as follows:**

Understanding Interest Rates: Be aware of how loans and savings accounts operate with interest. You can use this information to help you make wise choices regarding investments and borrowing.

Investment Fundamentals: Acquire knowledge of various investment opportunities, including stocks, bonds, and real estate. Gaining financial stability requires an understanding of risk and reward.

Tax Management: Recognize how your financial actions may affect your taxes. Over time, careful tax preparation can result in significant financial savings.

Putting Finances on Autopilot.

Automating your accounts can help you maintain a solid financial base. Establish automatic payments for bills, investments, and savings. Automation guarantees that you continuously strive toward your goals and makes it easy to stick to your financial strategy.

Observing and Modifying.

Building a strong financial base requires work and patience. It requires ongoing scrutiny and adjustment. Regularly assess your assets, savings, and budget to ensure that they all align with your financial goals. Make the required modifications to cope with life's and the economy's ups and downs.

Consultants and advisors in finance.

Working with a financial advisor or consultant can be a beneficial first step toward laying a strong financial foundation for some people. These experts can offer you advice and knowledge to help you attain your financial objectives and make wise decisions.

Your wealth will rise from the solid foundation of your financial situation. Through meticulous preparation of this foundation, you position yourself for prosperity and financial security in the future. We'll continue discussing the foundations of wealth and how they fit into your journey from rag to riches in the upcoming chapters.

Chapter 4

The Power of Budgeting and Saving.

Two essential skills in your financial toolbox are saving and budgeting. We'll explore the tremendous power these practices possess in this chapter, as well as how they can help you get from where you are to where you want to be.

Creating a Budget: Your Financial Guide.

You might think of a budget as your financial roadmap. It's a detailed plan that allocates your income to different expenses, savings, and goals related to money. ***This is why making a budget is crucial.***

1. Financial Clarity: Having a budget enables you to track your expenses. It helps you gain awareness of your spending patterns and pinpoint areas where you may make savings or increase your budget.

2. Goal Alignment: You may match your spending to your financial objectives by using your budget. Your budget guarantees that money is set aside for goals like investing for retirement or saving for a down payment on a home.

3. Debt Management: One effective strategy for paying off debt is budgeting. You can expedite and lower interest costs by setting aside more funds for debt repayment.

4. Emergency Preparedness: A well-organized budget calls for a contribution to an emergency fund. You may weather unforeseen expenses with this cash cushion without having to stop making progress toward your financial goals.

The Savings Craft:

Savings is the process of putting some of your money aside for later. It promotes wealth accumulation and acts as a cornerstone of economic stability. **This is the reason saving money is so important:**

1. Financial Security: A safety net is provided by savings. You're more equipped to handle unforeseen circumstances like auto repairs, medical problems, and job loss when you have money saved up.

2. Riches Creation: The foundation of riches is saved money. You can invest the money you save, which will allow compound interest to build your savings over time.

3. Opportunity Seizing: You can use your savings to take advantage of possibilities by buying a house, investing in a potential business, or going back to school.

Establishing and maintaining a budget

To make a budget, do the following:

1. Monitor Your Earnings and Outlays: Keep a record of all your spending and your sources of revenue. To help you stay organized, use tools like spreadsheets or apps for budgeting.

2. Sort Expenses: Put your costs in groups according to things like lodging, travel, groceries, entertainment, and savings.

3. Establish Financial Objectives: Identify your financial objectives, including short-, medium-, and long-term (e.g., vacation, down payment, and retirement).

4. Allocate Funds: Divide your earnings among your spending, savings, and financial objectives. Make sure that your costs stay within your revenue and that your budget is balanced.

5. Monitor and Modify: To keep tabs on your development, periodically evaluate your budget. Make the appropriate adjustments, particularly as circumstances change or unforeseen costs appear.

The Savings Pattern

Just as important as creating a budget is learning how to save. Begin by:

- Determining precise savings objectives, such as retirement, a vacation, or an emergency fund.
-Automating transfers to your investment or savings accounts to automate your savings
-cutting back on wasteful spending and putting the money saved.

Recall that disciplined and constant saving, regardless of the quantity, can eventually result in substantial financial development.

We'll look at several investing and savings techniques that can help you increase your wealth in the next chapters. Creating a budget and saving money are the first steps toward becoming financially successful, so start with these habits and see how your finances improve.

Chapter 5

Investing for Long-Term Growth.

One of the most effective methods you have to increase your wealth is investing. This chapter will discuss investing for long-term growth and how it can accelerate your ascent from rags to riches.

The investing power

The technique of using your money to generate returns over time is known as investing. It's a cornerstone wealth-building approach since it can increase your assets and beat inflation.

This explains why investing has such power:

1. Compound Growth: Your investments have the potential to generate more profits. Because of the compounding impact, your wealth may increase dramatically over time.

2. Outpacing Inflation: Savings in a traditional savings account may not be sufficient to keep up with inflation. Investing gives you the chance to grow your wealth faster than inflation.

3. Diversification: You can lower risk and possibly increase returns by investing by spreading your assets across a variety of investment types.

Long-Term Viewpoint.

Patience and an eye beyond immediate gains are necessary when investing for long-term prosperity. It means setting financial targets that may not be reached for years or perhaps decades. **These are crucial concepts to consider:**

1. Risk and Reward: Recognize that the degree of risk associated with various investments varies. Higher returns are often possible with riskier investments, but higher volatility is a possibility as well. Match your financial objectives and risk tolerance to your assets.

2. Diversify Your Holdings: Refrain from placing all of your money in one place. Spreading risk can be achieved by diversifying your investments among various asset types, including bonds, stocks, and real estate.

3. Buy and Hold: Purchasing high-quality investments and hanging onto them for an extended period can be a wise course of action. It's well known that timing the market is tough, and long-term investors typically do better.

4. Reinvest Returns and Dividends: Instead of spending dividends or interest you earn from your investments, reinvest them. Compounding gains more power as a result.

Investment-Grade Items.

For long-term growth, a variety of investment vehicles are available. *They could consist of:*

1. Stocks: A stake in a business that has the potential to grow in value and provide dividends.

2. Bonds: debt instruments that, upon maturity, return the principal amount plus interest at regular intervals.

3. Mutual funds: professionally managed pools of investments in a range of assets

4. Exchange-exchanged funds (ETFs): exchanged on an exchange like stocks but akin to mutual funds

5. Real Estate: Possession of tangible assets or investments in real estate trusts (REITs)

6. Retirement Accounts: These tax-advantaged accounts, such as IRAs or 401(k)s, are intended for long-term investment and savings.

Formulating a Financial Strategy.

Take these actions to invest for long-term growth:

1. Establish clear goals: Specify your financial goals, including retirement, house ownership, and school funding.

2. Evaluate Your Risk Tolerance: Based on your age, financial status, and aspirations, ascertain the level of risk you can tolerate.

3. Diversify Your Portfolio: To reduce risk, distribute your investments among several asset classes.

4. Regular Contributions: Invest a regular percentage of your money, either on a monthly or yearly basis.

5. Monitor and Modify: To keep your portfolio in line with your objectives and risk tolerance, periodically examine it and make any necessary adjustments.

The journey of investing is not without its ups and downs. It may, however, be a potent tool for achieving financial progress and securing your journey from rags to riches. if you have a long-term outlook and stick to your investment plan.

Chapter 6

Navigating the World of Real Estate.

One special and effective way to generate wealth is through real estate. We'll delve into the nuances of real estate in this chapter and see how it may be a key component of your journey from rags to riches.

The Benefits of Real Estate.

The allure of real estate investing as a wealth-building tactic is mostly due to its many benefits:

1. Appreciation: The value of real estate frequently increases over time, enabling you to accumulate equity.

2. Rental money: You can produce a consistent flow of money from your rental property, which can serve as a passive cash flow source.

3. Leverage: Investing in real estate allows you to use leverage. Buying real estate with a mortgage can increase your profits.

4. Tax Benefits: Investing in real estate frequently entails tax benefits such as depreciation, mortgage interest, and property tax deductions.

Real Estate Investment Types.

Investing in real estate can take many different forms.

1. Residential Real Estate: This category includes apartments, condominiums, and single-family homes. Residential properties are frequently rented out or used as personal residences.

2. Commercial Real Estate: Office buildings, retail establishments, and industrial properties are all considered commercial properties. Significant rental income and possible capital growth are two benefits of investing in commercial real estate.

3. Real Estate Investment Trusts (REITs): Investing in a diverse portfolio of real estate holdings is made possible through REITs. They provide a way to invest in real estate without actually owning any properties, and they are exchanged on stock exchanges.

4. Real Estate Crowdfunding: You can invest in real estate projects with comparatively low entrance costs by using crowdfunding platforms. To finance real estate ventures, you can collaborate with other investors.

Important things to remember.

Before getting started in real estate, it's critical to comprehend the following:

1. Location Is Important: When buying real estate, location is important. Invest in communities with room to grow, low crime rates, excellent educational opportunities, and features that draw in renters and buyers.

2. Property Type: Think about the kind of real estate you wish to purchase. Single-family homes could be a good source of passive income, while commercial real estate could yield larger returns but need more upkeep.

3. Market study: To comprehend property valuations, rental rates, and demand in your selected area, carry out an in-depth market study.

4. Financing: Make sure you obtain financing with advantageous conditions if you require a mortgage.

5. Property Management: Take into account if you want to work with a property management company or handle the property yourself.

Rewards and Risks.

Investing in real estate carries some risks as well as advantages. Even though there is a chance for large returns, it's important to understand the difficulties:

1. Market Volatility: Changes in the real estate market can have an impact on rental income and property values.

2. Property Management: It can be difficult and time-consuming to oversee tenants and maintain a property.

3. Liquidity: Investing in real estate is not liquid. Property sales may require a lengthy process and incur transaction fees.

4. Risk management: Reduce risk by spreading out your real estate holdings and making sure you have enough cash on hand to cover unforeseen costs.

A Tool for Creating Wealth.

A tool for accumulating wealth that can improve your financial portfolio is real estate. Real estate investing requires a well-thought-out plan and a long-term outlook, regardless of whether you want to invest in residential, commercial, REIT, or real estate crowdfunding. Real estate can be a key component of your journey from rags to riches if you navigate it carefully.

Chapter 7

Entrepreneurship and Wealth Creation.

A dynamic and transformational route to generating wealth is through entrepreneurship. We'll look at the world of entrepreneurship in this chapter, along with its special benefits and how it can help you get from rags to riches.

The Benefits of Entrepreneurship

The following are the main benefits of entrepreneurship as a wealth-building tactic:

1. Unlimited Potential: You have the chance to start and expand your own company as an entrepreneur, and the potential for financial gain is limitless.

2. Control: Business owners have more power over their financial future. Their company and financial results are strongly impacted by the decisions they make.

3. Passion and Purpose: A lot of business owners are motivated by their love of what they do and a desire to leave a lasting impression. This has the potential to be a strong success motivator.

4. Multiple Income Streams: Via their company endeavors, successful entrepreneurs can generate several revenue streams, which can offer financial stability and diversification.

Important Entrepreneurship Ideas.

Before pursuing entrepreneurship as a means of generating money, take into account these fundamental ideas:

1. Identify Opportunities: Finding market opportunities or issues that your company can solve is frequently the first step in entrepreneurship.

2. Draft a Business Plan: Write a thorough business plan that details your idea, target market, competitors, and projected financials.

3. Execution and Persistence: Developing an idea into a profitable company requires commitment, diligence, and the capacity to keep going in the face of difficulties.

4. Financial Management: A company's ability to successfully manage its finances is essential. This covers cash flow management, accounting, and budgeting.

5. Innovation and Adaptation: The environment in which businesses operate is always evolving. To be competitive, successful entrepreneurs must maintain their inventiveness and flexibility.

6. Assemble a Powerful Team: Assemble a knowledgeable and driven group of people who can assist you in realizing your company's goals.

Types of Business Ventures.

There are several types of entrepreneurship. *These are a few typical kinds:*

1. Small company entrepreneurship: establishing and managing a small company, frequently in a local or specialized market.

2. Startup Entrepreneurship: starting a business with the potential for rapid growth and offering cutting-edge goods or services.

3. Franchising Entrepreneurship: Purchasing and running a franchise of a well-known company

4. Internet-based entrepreneurship: using the web to develop and promote goods and services

5. Social Entrepreneurship: applying business acumen to a cause that aims to improve the environment or society.

Rewards and Risks.

Being an entrepreneur comes with dangers. *It's critical to understand the difficulties:*

1. Financial Risk: There is a chance that a business will fail if a large financial investment is made during its startup and operation.

2. Uncertainty: The entrepreneurial journey is frequently uncertain, and success is not always assured. Your firm may be impacted by unanticipated events, competition, and changes in the market.

3. Work-Life Balance: Particularly in the early phases of company development, entrepreneurs may find it difficult to strike a balance between their personal and professional lives.

4. Accountability: As the company's proprietor, you bear the responsibility for the prosperity and expansion of your enterprise.

The Path of an Entrepreneur.

Although it comes with hazards, entrepreneurship may be a life-changing experience that also has the potential to yield large benefits. Wealth is created by prosperous businesspeople not only for themselves but also frequently for their communities and staff. When you're on a journey from rags to riches, entrepreneurship may be a powerful route to wealth creation and financial freedom, regardless of whether you're creating a small firm, a tech startup, or a social impact enterprise.

Chapter 8
Managing Debt Wisely.

Debt can be a double-edged sword. When handled effectively, it can help you reach your financial goals, but when mismanaged, it can become a huge hurdle. In this chapter, we'll study the skill of managing debt properly and how it plays a critical role in your journey from rags to riches.

The good and bad of debt.

Debt is not necessarily good or evil; it's a financial tool. Understanding the distinction between good debt and bad debt is the foundation of wise debt management.

Good Debt: Good debt is often utilized to invest in assets that can appreciate or provide income. **Examples include:**

•mortgage debt for a home, which can rise in value.
•Student loans for schooling can lead to increased earning potential.
•business loans to start or expand a business that generates income.

Bad Debt: Bad debt is employed for consumption or expenditures that do not contribute to your financial well-being. **Examples include:**

•high-interest credit card debt for non-essential expenditures.
•loans for depreciating assets like cars, which lose value over time.
•personal loans for frivolous expenses.

Strategies for managing debt.

1. Create a Debt Repayment Plan: Begin by listing all your debts, including the outstanding sums, interest rates, and minimum payments. Develop a debt repayment plan that allocates extra income to pay off high-interest debt first.

2. Prioritize High-Interest Debt: High-interest debt, such as credit card debt, should be a priority. The high interest rates make it pricier in the long term.

3. Budget for Debt Repayment: Include debt repayment as a budget area to ensure you devote funds to it each month.

4. Snowball or Avalanche approach: Consider utilizing the debt snowball approach (paying off the smallest debt first) or the debt avalanche method (paying off the highest interest debt first) based on your psychological and financial preferences.

5. Debt Consolidation: In some situations, combining high-interest debt into a lower-interest loan might help you save money and simplify your payments.

6. Avoid New Debt: While repaying existing debt, avoid amassing new debt to keep your financial condition from worsening.

Using Debt for Investment.

It's vital to recognize that borrowing debt for investment objectives can be a sensible financial decision. When you invest borrowed money in assets that appreciate or create income at a rate higher than the interest on the debt, you can leverage your way to riches.

For example, acquiring a mortgage to acquire real estate, starting a business with a loan, or using margin debt for stock transactions can potentially provide big returns.

However, this method demands careful risk assessment and a clear grasp of the potential rewards and repercussions.

Building a Debt-Free Future.

The ultimate goal of good debt management is to work toward a debt-free future. By meticulously following a debt repayment plan and making sensible financial decisions, you may free yourself from the burden of debt and redirect your resources to wealth-building possibilities.

Managing debt correctly is not just about getting out of debt; it's about setting yourself up for financial success. Your road from rags to riches becomes smoother and more feasible when you're in charge of your financial commitments and making informed choices about when to use debt as a strategic tool.

Chapter 9

Protecting Your Wealth: Insurance and Risk Management.

In your journey from rags to riches, one of the most crucial aspects is safeguarding the fortune you've built. To motivate you on this path, consider the wise words of Warren Buffett, one of the most successful business titans of our time:

"Trouble comes from not knowing what you're doing." **Wayne Buffett**

In this chapter, we'll discuss the role of insurance and risk management in conserving and protecting your hard-earned assets.

The Importance of Risk Management.

Life is fundamentally uncertain, and financial hazards abound. To secure your wealth, it's vital to establish a complete risk management approach. **This technique includes:**

1. Insurance: To protect against financial losses from unanticipated catastrophes.
2. Emergency Funds: To cover unforeseen bills and crises without derailing your financial plans.
3. Diversification: spreading your investments across several asset types to lessen risk.
4. Estate planning: ensuring that your assets are allocated according to your intentions and that your loved ones are protected in the event of your incapacity or passing.

Types of Insurance.

1. Health Insurance: Provides coverage for medical expenses, guaranteeing that you have access to healthcare without incurring extravagant fees.

2. Life insurance: It protects your family and beneficiaries financially in the event of your death. It can cover funeral expenses, debt payback, and financial support.

3. Auto Insurance: Mandatory for vehicle owners in many places, it covers damages and responsibility in case of accidents.

4. Homeowners or Renters Insurance: Protects your home or valuables from harm or theft. It also provides liability coverage.

5. Disability Insurance: Provides income replacement if you're unable to work due to disability or illness.

6. Long-Term Care Insurance: Covers expenses connected to long-term care, such as nursing homes or in-home care, which are not normally covered by health insurance.

7. Umbrella Insurance: Offers supplementary liability coverage that goes beyond the limits of previous plans. It's especially valuable for those with considerable holdings.

Evaluating Your Insurance Needs.

To choose the correct insurance coverage, evaluate your personal and financial circumstances.

Assess Your Hazards: Identify the potential hazards you face, such as health difficulties, auto accidents, property damage, or premature mortality.
Review Existing Coverage: Understand the insurance policies you already have in place and their coverage restrictions.
Set a Budget: Determine how much you can allocate to insurance premiums while maintaining your other financial goals.
Work with an Insurance Advisor: Consult an insurance specialist or advisor to assist you in assessing your needs and identifying suitable plans.

Managing Risks Beyond Insurance.

Risk management goes beyond insurance. It involves efforts to reduce or manage potential risks.

Emergency Funds: Building and maintaining an emergency fund to cover unforeseen needs can lessen financial shocks.
Asset Diversification: Diversifying your investments can help spread risk and decrease the impact of market swings.
Estate Planning: Proper estate planning guarantees that your assets are handled and dispersed according to your intentions.
Legal Protections: Implement legal protections such as wills, trusts, and powers of attorney to secure your interests.

Continuous Review.

As your financial condition and aspirations vary, it's necessary to reassess your risk management and insurance plans. Regular assessments with financial advisors or insurance specialists can assist in ensuring that your insurance coverage remains aligned with your requirements and circumstances.

Protecting your capital with insurance and risk management is a crucial element of your financial journey. It ensures that you and your family are protected in the face of unanticipated occurrences and provides the peace of mind to continue striving for financial success and wealth growth.

Chapter 10
The Art of Giving Back.

On your path from rags to riches, it's not just about amassing cash; it's also about making a beneficial impact on the world. This chapter looks into the art of giving back, the profound value of charity, and the fulfillment it offers.

The transformative power of giving.

The act of giving is a strong force for transformation, not just in the lives of those who receive but also in the hearts of those who give. It's a reminder that wealth, when utilized intelligently, can be a force for good.

1. Personal Fulfillment: Giving back brings a strong sense of fulfillment and purpose. It's an acknowledgment of the difference you can make in the lives of people and your community.

2. Influence: By contributing to charitable organizations or initiatives, you can have a major influence on topics that are important to you, whether it's education, healthcare, poverty reduction, or environmental conservation.

3. Legacy: Philanthropy helps you leave a lasting legacy. Your gifts can continue to benefit generations long after you're gone.

Ways to Give Back.

1. Charitable Donations: Direct contributions to non-profit organizations or causes you're enthusiastic about.

2. Volunteerism: giving your time, skills, and knowledge to help those in need or to promote community efforts.

3. Foundations: Establishing your foundation to allocate resources toward specified causes

4. Impact investing: investing in enterprises or businesses that attempt to produce beneficial social or environmental change while simultaneously creating financial gains.

5. Mentorship: sharing your expertise and experiences with others and encouraging them toward success.

The Ripple Effect.

One act of giving can start a ripple effect, prompting others to do the same. This concerted effort can lead to revolutionary transformations in communities and beyond. As you acquire and grow your fortune, remember the words of Andrew Carnegie, one of history's greatest philanthropists:

"The man who dies rich dies disgraced." **Andrew Carnegie.**

This remark reminds us that obtaining wealth is not enough; how you use your wealth to assist others and create a better world is equally essential. Embrace the art of giving back, for it is a meaningful element of your journey from rags to riches and leaves a legacy that goes far beyond financial gain.

CONCLUSION.

Your path from poverty to wealth has served as an investigation of the ideas and tactics that lead to affluent living. Recall that building a prosperous life involves creating a life that is abundant, secure, and fulfilling rather than just acquiring cash.

Start with an idea that motivates your financial objectives. Develop a wealth-oriented attitude to start building your future finances. Accept the value of saving, investing, and creating a budget. Discover the world of entrepreneurship and learn how to utilize debt strategically. Use insurance to reduce risk and safeguard your assets.

True wealth, however, goes beyond mere acquisition. It's about leaving a legacy, impacting the world, and giving back. Remember the richness that diversity adds to your financial fabric when you look back on your path.

The journey to financial success involves more than simply getting where you're going; it also involves appreciating every step you take. I hope and pray that your path brings you prosperity, influence, and true happiness. I appreciate you allowing me to join you on this financial journey. Cheers to your reaching financial success!

www.ingramcontent.com/pod-product-compliance
Lightning Source LLC
Chambersburg PA
CBHW072228290526
45794CB00007B/2929